W9-DDU-124

GIFTED
&
TALENTED®

*To develop*
*your child's gifts*
*and talents*

# PHONICS

## A Workbook for Ages 4-6

Written by Martha Cheney
Illustrated by Kerry Manwaring

Lowell House
Juvenile
Los Angeles

CONTEMPORARY BOOKS
Chicago

Requests for such permissions should be addressed to:
Lowell House Juvenile
2020 Avenue of the Stars, Suite 300
Los Angeles, CA 90067

Lowell House books can be purchased at special discounts when ordered in bulk for
premiums and special sales. Contact Department TC at the above address.

Manufactured in the United States of America

ISBN: 1-56565-365-3

10  9  8  7

**GIFTED & TALENTED® WORKBOOKS** will help develop your child's natural talents and gifts by providing activities to enhance critical and creative thinking skills. These skills of logic and reasoning teach children **how** to think. They are precisely the skills emphasized by teachers of gifted and talented children.

Thinking skills are the skills needed to be able to learn anything at any time. Unlike events, words, and teaching methods, thinking skills never change. If a child has a grasp of how to think, school success and even success in life will become more assured. In addition, the child will become self-confident as he or she approaches new tasks with the ability to think them through and discover solutions.

**GIFTED & TALENTED® WORKBOOKS** present these skills in a unique way, combining the basic subject areas of reading, language arts, and math with thinking skills. The top of each page is labeled to indicate the specific thinking skill developed. Here are some of the skills you will find:

- Deduction—the ability to reach a logical conclusion by interpreting clues
- Understanding Relationships—the ability to recognize how objects, shapes, and words are similar or dissimilar; to classify or categorize
- Sequencing—the ability to organize events, numbers; to recognize patterns
- Inference—the ability to reach a logical conclusion from given or assumed evidence
- Creative Thinking—the ability to generate unique ideas; to compare and contrast the same elements in different situations; to present imaginative solutions to problems

**GIFTED & TALENTED® WORKBOOKS** have been written by teachers. Educationally sound and endorsed by leaders in the gifted field, this series will benefit any child who demonstrates curiosity, imagination, a sense of fun and wonder about the world, and a desire to learn. These books will open your child's mind to new experiences and help fulfill his or her true potential.

This book is designed to give children an opportunity to play with and explore the sounds of the letters of the alphabet. This study of the letter sounds is known as **phonics**.

Almost every page asks the child to write or draw in response to the challenge or question presented. This helps to put the task of working with letters in context. The importance of phonics lies in its ability to help us to understand and express language, so in addition to decoding, the child is expected to demonstrate understanding and practice expression. If this proves difficult for your child, don't be afraid to help. Encourage him or her to talk through the responses while thinking them through. If your child has not yet mastered writing, allow him or her to dictate longer answers while you write them. Write slowly, and let your child watch as you form the letters. Together, read back your child's own words.

The activities should be done consecutively, as they become increasingly challenging as the book progresses. Notice that on many pages, there is more than one right answer. Accept your child's response and then challenge him or her to come up with another. Also, where the child is asked to write, remember that the expression of his or her ideas is more important than spelling. At this age, the child should be encouraged to record the letter sounds that he or she hears without fear of mistakes. This process is known as **invented spelling**. If children only write words they know they can spell correctly, they will limit their written expression. Using invented spelling permits your child's spoken vocabulary to be available to him or her for writing. This vocabulary is vastly greater than the list of words that a five- or six-year-old can spell correctly.

For example, if your child writes *dnosr* for *dinosaur*, that's okay! Praise your child for the sounds he or she heard. You can encourage the child to listen for the missing vowels as you say the word and write it out so that the child can see the correct form. Just keep the emphasis on his or her success—the letters your child did hear—and not on his or her "error." The youngster needs to grow in confidence and exhibit curiosity about the sounds of the letters and how they go together to make words. The experience of attempting new words requires careful thought about the sounds of the letters and makes them more and more the explorer's own.

Reference charts depicting the sounds of letters appear on the next few pages. Help your child use the charts whenever he or she needs a reminder.

# Consonant Chart

**b** banana

**h** hat

**c** cat

**j** jar

**d** dog

**k** kite

**f** fish

**l** lion

**g** girl

**m** moon

**n** nest

**p** penguin

**q** queen

**r** raccoon

**s** sun

**t** telephone

**v** violin

**w** wagon

**x** X ray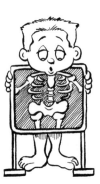

**y** yarn

**z** zebra

# Vowel Chart

| **Short Vowel Sounds at the Beginning of Words** | **Long Vowel Sounds at the Beginning of Words** |
|---|---|

**a** apple

**a** acorn

**e** elephant

**e** eagle

**i** iguana

**i** ice

**o** octopus

**o** ocean

**u** umbrella

**u** unicorn

# Vowel Chart

| **Short Vowel Sounds Within Words** | **Long Vowel Sounds Within Words** |
|---|---|

**a** cat

**a** cake

**e** bed

**e** jeep

**i** pig

**i** bike

**o** fox

**o** boat

**u** bug

**u** cube

Fill in the missing consonant in each word. Tell a story about each picture.

a __oy with a __og

a __at in a __ox

a __at on a __og

Fill in each missing letter. Use the pictures to help you decide which letter is missing. Now read the words out loud. Notice that all the words have short vowel sounds. What else do you notice about the words?

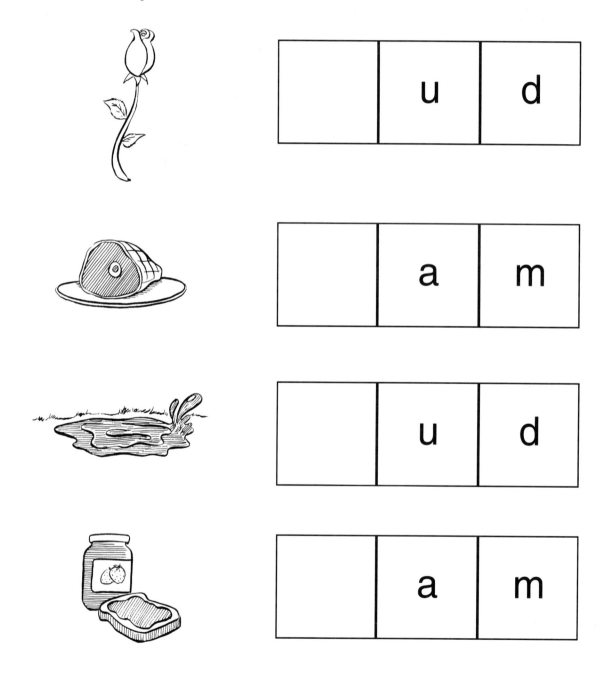

| | u | d |
|---|---|---|

| | a | m |
|---|---|---|

| | u | d |
|---|---|---|

| | a | m |
|---|---|---|

# Look, Listen, and Write

Look at each picture. What do you see? Say the word. Write the letter that makes the beginning sound of the word. What other letter sounds can you hear when you say this word? Try to spell the word using the sounds you hear. The first one has been done for you.

bug

In what way are all of these things the same? Say your answer out loud.

Fill in the missing consonant in each word. Tell a story about each picture.

a __ad in a __an

a __up in the __un

a __ox with a __at

Draw a line from each word to the object that shows what that word means. Some words might go with more than one object. Some objects might go with more than one word.

**key**                                                    **cup**

**hot**                                                    **pet**

**cat**                                                    **fish**

# The Land of J

Welcome to the Land of J. Many things in this world begin with the letter **J**. Circle them all. Think of more objects that might be found in the Land of J. Use the lines at the bottom of the page to list them.

_____     _____

_ _ _ _ _ _ _ _ _ _ _ _ _ _ _ _     _ _ _ _ _ _ _ _ _ _ _ _ _ _ _ _

_____     _____

_____     _____

_ _ _ _ _ _ _ _ _ _ _ _ _ _ _ _     _ _ _ _ _ _ _ _ _ _ _ _ _ _ _ _

_____     _____

Fill in each missing letter. Use the pictures to help you decide which letter is missing. Now read the words out loud. Notice that all the words have short vowel sounds. Do any of these words rhyme?

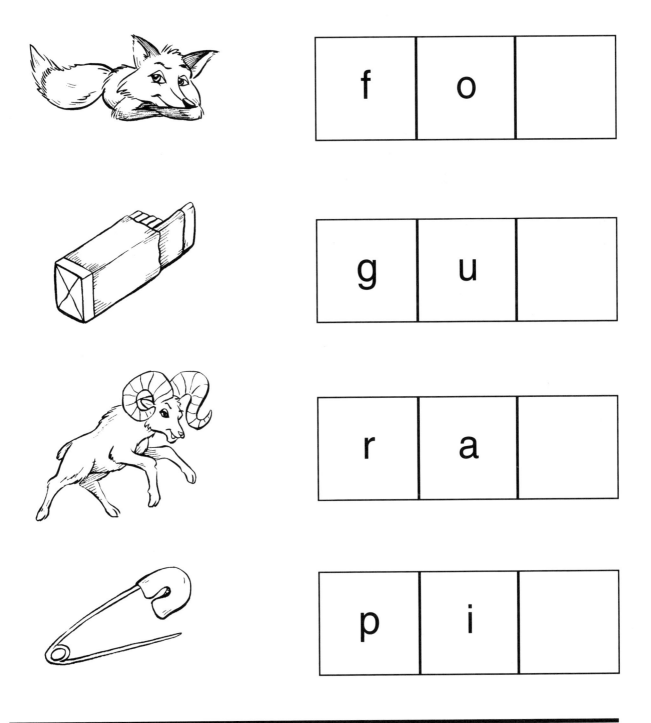

| f | o | |
|---|---|---|

| g | u | |
|---|---|---|

| r | a | |
|---|---|---|

| p | i | |
|---|---|---|

# Look, Listen, and Write

Look at each picture. What do you see? Say the word. Write the letter that makes the beginning sound of the word. What other letter sounds can you hear when you say this word? Try to spell the word using the sounds you hear.

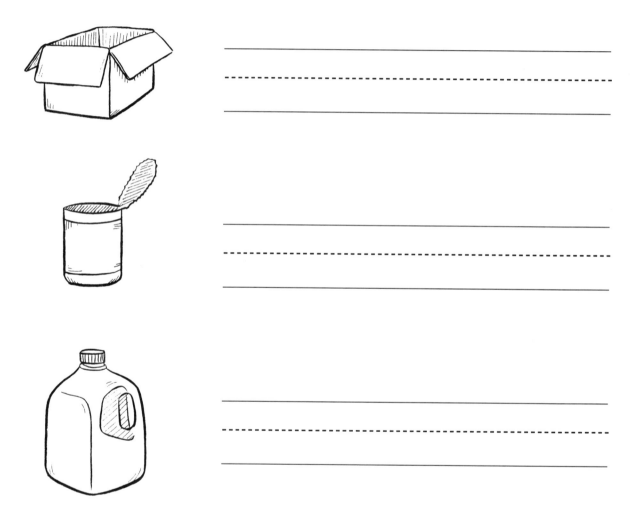

In what way are all of these things the same? Say your answer out loud.

## The Land of T

Welcome to the Land of T. Many things in this world begin with the letter **T**. Circle them all. Think of more objects that might be found in the Land of T. Use the lines at the bottom of the page to list them.

_____    _____

------------------------    ------------------------

_____    _____

_____    _____

------------------------    ------------------------

_____    _____

Each of these words is missing a short vowel. Fill in each
missing letter. Use the pictures to help you decide which
letter is missing. Use each letter only once. Think of
another word with a short vowel sound. Say that word
out loud.

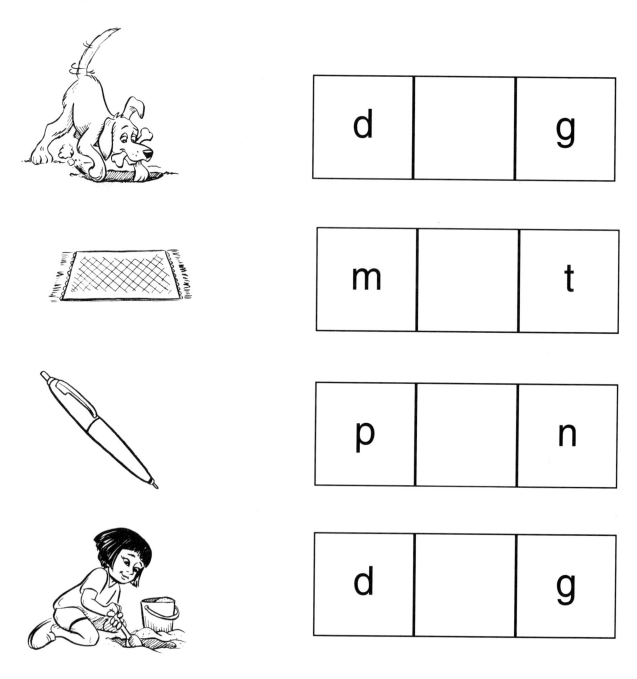

| d | | g |
|---|---|---|

| m | | t |
|---|---|---|

| p | | n |
|---|---|---|

| d | | g |
|---|---|---|

Each of these words is missing a short vowel. Fill in each missing letter. Use the pictures to help you decide which letter is missing. Use each letter only once. Think of another word with a short vowel sound. Say that word out loud.

| m | | g |
|---|---|---|

| p | | n |
|---|---|---|

| p | | t |
|---|---|---|

| t | | n |
|---|---|---|

Draw a line from each word to the object that shows what that word means. Some words might go with more than one object. Some objects might go with more than one word.

cap

hat

mad

man

king

bug

Draw a picture above each group of words to show what the words say.

a big bug

a sad dad

a red pet

a wet mop

Draw a picture above each group of words to show what the words say.

ten dots

a tot on a bus

a fat fox

a hot dog

# The Land of W

Welcome to the Land of W. Many things in this world begin with the letter **W**. Circle them all. Think of more objects that might be found in the Land of W. Use the lines at the bottom of the page to list them.

_____    _____

-------------------------    -------------------------

_____    _____

_____    _____

-------------------------    -------------------------

_____    _____

Draw a line from each word to the object that shows what that word means. Some words might go with more than one object. Some objects might go with more than one word.

**bat**  **big**

**nut**  **ball**

**bag**  **net**

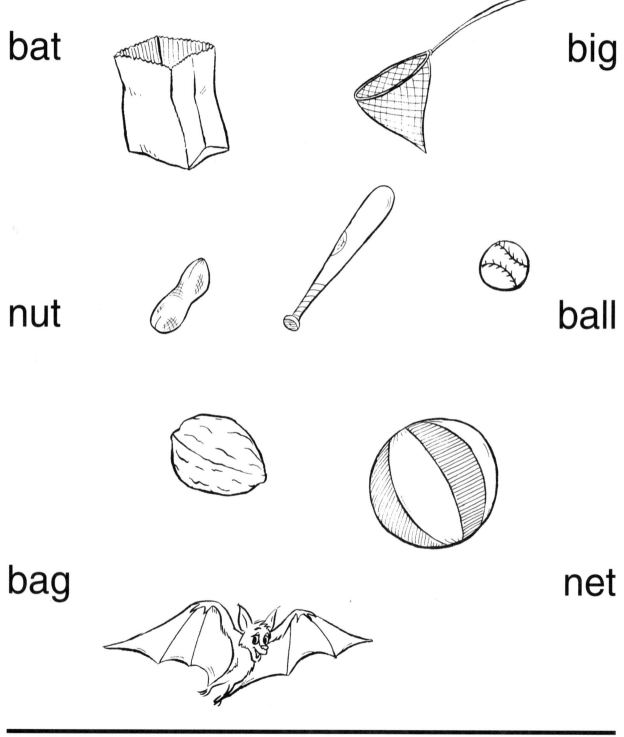

# The Land of L

Welcome to the Land of L. Many things in this world begin with the letter **L**. Circle them all. Think of more objects that might be found in the Land of L. Use the lines at the bottom of the page to list them.

_____        _____

- - - - - - - - - - - - - - - - - - -        - - - - - - - - - - - - - - - - - - -

_____        _____

_____        _____

- - - - - - - - - - - - - - - - - - -        - - - - - - - - - - - - - - - - - - -

_____        _____

Fill in the blank with any letter that will form a word that makes sense. Then draw a picture that illustrates the word.

__an

__ip

__ot

__ing

__ox

__it

Fill in the blank with any letter that will form a word that makes sense. Then draw a picture that illustrates the word.

__at

__og

__ish

__et

__and

__op

In each set of words, the same long vowel is missing. Fill in the missing vowel in each group.

| h__le | b__ke | r__al |
| m__le | M__ke | m__al |
| p__le | h__ke | st__al |
| b__wl | l__ke | s__al |

The words in each group rhyme with each other. Have an adult help you make up a poem using some of the rhyming words.

_____

_____

_____

_____

All of the objects on this page have a long vowel sound. Color all of the objects with the long **a** sound red. Color all of the objects with the long **e** sound green. Say the name of each object out loud.

In each set of words, the same long vowel is missing. Fill in the missing vowel in each group.

| c__ke | b__at | r__ce |
| l__ke | m__at | m__ce |
| m__ke | g__at | n__ce |
| b__ke | fl__at | sp__ce |

The words in each group rhyme with each other. Have an adult help you make up a poem using some of the rhyming words.

_____

_____

_____

_____

All of the objects on this page have a long vowel sound. Color all of the objects with the long **i** sound purple. Color all of the objects with the long **o** sound yellow. Color all of the objects with the long **u** sound blue. Say the name of each object out loud.

In each set of words, the same long vowel is missing. Fill in the missing vowel in each group.

| b__at | r__de | g__te |
| h__at | s__de | m__te |
| m__at | t__de | pl__te |
| n__at | h__de | d__te |

The words in each group rhyme with each other. Have an adult help you make up a poem using some of the rhyming words.

_____

_____

_____

_____

# Look, Listen, and Write

Look at each picture. What do you see? Say the word. Write the letter that makes the beginning sound of the word. What other letter sounds can you hear when you say this word? Try to spell the word using the sounds you hear.

In what way are all of these things the same? Say your answer out loud.

## Look, Listen, and Write

Look at each picture. What do you see? Say the word. Write the letter that makes the beginning sound of the word. What other letter sounds can you hear when you say this word? Try to spell the word using the sounds you hear.

In what way are all of these things the same? Say your answer out loud.

Draw a picture above each group of words to show what the words say.

a cube of ice

a game of tag

a red kite

a bean in a bowl

Read the words in the boxes. Look at the pictures. Color the pictures that show what the words say.

| a sad dog | a cold cat |
|---|---|

Fill in the blank with any letter that will form a word that makes sense. Then draw a picture that illustrates the word.

__ite

__og

__ake

__oat

__an

__ine

Draw a line from each word to the object that shows what that word means. Some words might go with more than one object. Some objects might go with more than one word.

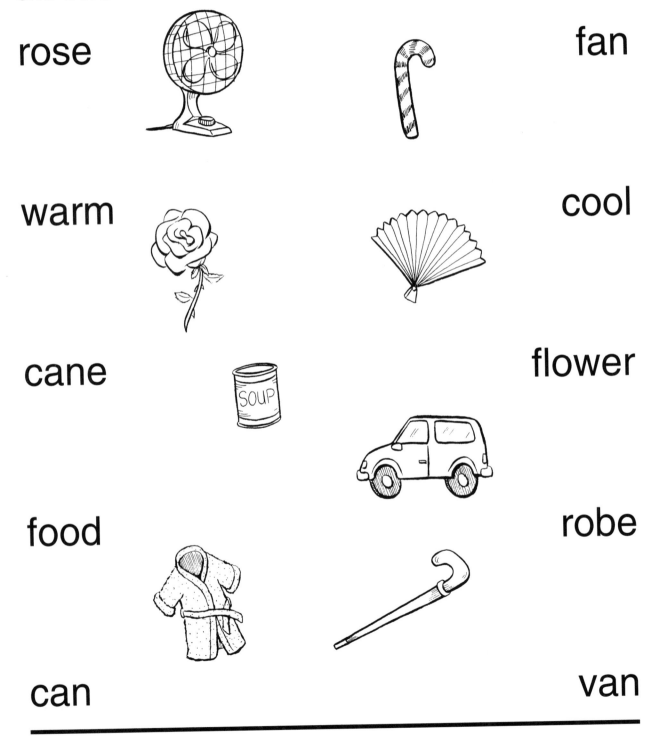

rose

fan

warm

cool

cane

flower

food

robe

can

van

In the first two boxes, fill in the blanks with consonants so that each sentence makes sense. The pictures will help you. In the last box, write a sentence and draw a picture to complete the story.

Here is a yam for __ou!

Is it __ummy?

Read the words in the boxes. Look at the pictures. Color the pictures that show what the words say.

| a fat frog | a wet goat |
|---|---|

Read the words in the boxes. Look at the pictures. Color the pictures that show what the words say.

| a nice mouse | a big ball |
|---|---|

Look at the picture in each box. Fill in the missing letter combination to form the word that describes each picture.

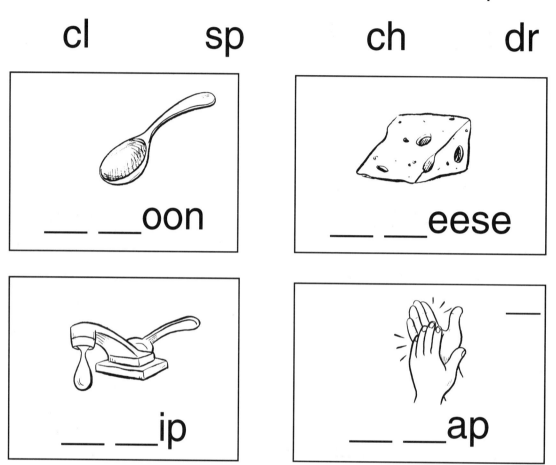

Draw a circle around the pictures whose names contain a short vowel sound. Then write a couple of sentences using all of the words that go with the pictures.

_____

_____

_____

_____

Look at the picture in each box. Fill in the missing letter combination to form the word that describes each picture.

sn      dr      sl      br

___ ___ess

___ ___ow

___ ___ide

___ ___oom

Draw a circle around the pictures whose names contain a short vowel sound. Then write a couple of sentences using all of the words that go with the pictures.

_____

_____

_____

_____

Draw a picture above each group of words to show what the words say.

a cake
on a plate

a ride
on a bike

a goat
in a boat

a snake
on a rake

Look at the picture. Fill in the missing letter combinations to form the words that describe the picture.

## fr        fl        cr        cl

__ __ock    __ __ag    __ __ow    __ __og

Draw a circle around the pictures whose names contain a short vowel sound. Then write a couple of sentences about the picture using all of the words that describe it.

_____

_____

_____

_____

Look at the picture. Fill in the missing letter combinations to form the words that describe the picture.

**sh**      **wh**      **tr**      **gr**

__ __ee      __ __ale      __ __ __eep      __ __ass

Draw a circle around the pictures whose names contain a short vowel sound. Then write a couple of sentences about the picture using all of the words that describe it.

_____

_____

_____

_____

Look for the pairs of objects whose names rhyme because they have the same ending. Draw a line between each rhyming pair.

Write a couple of sentences that tell about the picture. Say the words out loud. What vowel sounds do you hear? Underline each word that contains a short vowel sound.

_____

_____

_____

_____

Finish each sentence with a word that ends with **op**. Make sure each sentence makes sense! Then read the words out loud. Does the **o** in the words have a long or short vowel sound? What else do you notice about these words?

You wash the floor with a _____.

The opposite of bottom is _____.

A red light tells you to _____.

We go to the store to _____.

Finish each sentence with a word that ends with **an**. Make sure each sentence makes sense! Then read the words out loud. Does the **a** in the words have a long or short vowel sound? What else do you notice about these words?

Soup might be bought in a _____.

When it's hot, we turn on a _____.

Some people drive in a _____.

A light brown color is _____.

Look for the pairs of objects whose names rhyme because they have the same ending. Draw a line between each rhyming pair.

Write a couple of sentences that tell about the picture. Say the words out loud. What vowel sounds do you hear? Underline each word that contains a short vowel sound.

_____

_____

_____

_____

Finish each sentence with a word that ends with **et**. Make sure each sentence makes sense!

If you jump in a pool, you get _____.

When you play tennis, you hit the ball over a _____.

An animal you love is your_____.

Things that belong together make a _____.

Finish each sentence with a word that ends with **ish**. Make sure each sentence makes sense!

When you blow out the candles, you make a _____.

You can use a hook and a worm to catch a _____.

A plate for food is called a _____.

In each box, fill in the blanks with vowels so that the sentence makes sense. Draw a picture that shows what the sentence is about.

The f__sh can sw__m
in the p__nd.

The m__n h__t the b__ll
with the b__t.

In the first two boxes, fill in the blanks with consonants so that each sentence makes sense. The pictures will help you. In the last box, write a sentence and draw a picture to complete the story.

__ip up your __acket and

we will go to the __oo.

I __ __ink there is

a __ebra there.

In the first two boxes, fill in the blanks with consonants so that each sentence makes sense. The pictures will help you. In the last box, write a sentence and draw a picture to complete the story.

| The __oy sat on the __ug with his __at. | The __irl and the __ __ppy __an into the __oom. |

In the first two boxes, fill in the blanks with consonants so that each sentence makes sense. The pictures will help you. In the last box, write a sentence and draw a picture to complete the story.

A __an went for a

__alk in the __ark.

It was __ark and he

__ell into a __ole.

In the first two boxes, fill in the blanks with vowels so that each sentence makes sense. The pictures will help you. In the last box, write a sentence and draw a picture to complete the story.

The m __ce like to

sk__te on the __ce.

They have f__n in the

sn__w, but it is c__ld.

In the first two boxes, fill in the blanks with consonants or vowels so that each sentence makes sense. The pictures will help you. In the last box, write a sentence and draw a picture to complete the story.

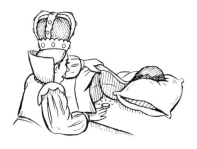

The __ __een is

being __ __iet.

She __ides a __ __arter

under the __ __ilt.

Write a story about the picture in the box. Say the words you want to use out loud and write down what you hear.

Write a story about the picture in the box. Say the words you want to use out loud and write down what you hear.

_____

_____

_____

_____

_____

_____

_____

_____

Write a story about the picture in the box. Say the words you want to use out loud and write down what you hear.

_____

_____

_____

_____

_____

_____

_____

_____

Write a story about the picture in the box. Say the words you want to use out loud and write down what you hear.

# Answers

**Page 9**
a boy with a dog
a rat in a box
a cat on a log

**Page 10**
bud, ham, mud, jam
The words are rhyming pairs.

**Page 11**
bug, dog, fox
They are all animals.
They all have legs.

**Page 12**
a dad in a van
a pup in the sun
a fox with a hat

**Page 13**

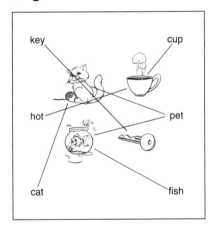

**Page 14**
jump rope, jail, jelly beans,
jam, jeep, judge, jewels,
jack-in-the-box, jackhammer,
junk, juice, jug
Additional answers will vary.

**Page 15**
fox, gum, ram, pin
The words do not rhyme.

**Page 16**
box, can, jug
They are all containers.

**Page 17**
tower, tigers, tennis, tennis
rackets, TV, telephone, tape,
typewriter, turkey, tent, trunk
Additional answers will vary.

**Page 18**
dog, mat, pen, dig

**Page 19**
mug, pan, pot, ten

**Page 20**

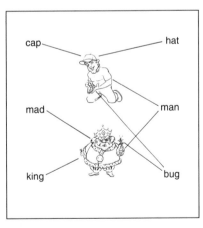

**Page 21**
*Parent:* Pictures should
show that child understands
the words.
Answers will vary.

**Page 22**
*Parent:* Pictures should
show that child understands
the words.
Answers will vary.

**Page 23**
wizard, wall, watermelons,
wagon, water, wrench, wood,
wigwams, wolf, walrus,
windmill
Additional answers will vary.

**Page 24**

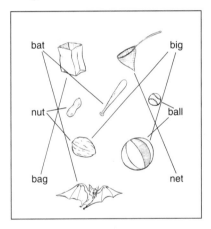

**Page 25**
lemons, lantern, lion,
lighthouse, lock, lobster,
ladder, lamb, leaves
Additional answers will vary.

**Page 26**
Answers will vary.

**Page 27**
Answers will vary.

**Page 28**
o, i, e
Rhymes will vary.

**Page 29**

| long a | long e |
|--------|--------|
| plane  | cheese |
| rain   | beach  |
| cage   | heel   |
| face   | key    |
| gate   | leaf   |
| tape   | meat   |

**Page 30**
a, o, i
Rhymes will vary.

**Page 31**

| long i | long o | long u |
|--------|--------|--------|
| bike   | coat   | cube   |
| kite   | rose   | tuba   |
| knife  | soap   | mule   |
| tiger  |        |        |

**Page 32**
e, i, a
Rhymes will vary.

**Page 33**
face, nose, toe
They are all parts of the body.

**Page 34**
shirt, shoe, sock
They are all articles of clothing.

**Page 35**
*Parent:* Pictures should show that child understands the words.
Answers will vary.

**Page 36**
The sad dog should be colored in.
The cold cat should be colored in.

**Page 37**
*Parent:* Pictures should show that child understands the words.
Answers will vary.

**Page 38**

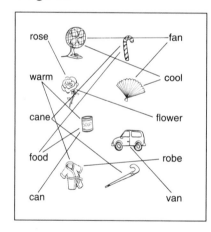

**Page 39**
Here is a yam for you.
Is it yummy?
Rest of answer will vary.

**Page 40**
The fat frog should be colored in.
The wet goat should be colored in.

**Page 41**
The nice mouse should be colored in.
The big ball should be colored in.

**Page 42**
spoon, cheese, drip, clap
**Drip** and **clap** have short vowel sounds.
Rest of answer will vary.

**Page 43**
dress, snow, slide, broom
**Dress** has a short vowel sound.
Rest of answer will vary.

**Page 44**
*Parent:* Pictures should show that child understands the words.
Answers will vary.

**Page 45**
clock, flag, crow, frog
**Clock, flag,** and **frog** have short vowel sounds.
Rest of answer will vary.

**Page 46**
tree, whale, sheep, grass
**Grass** has a short vowel sound.
Rest of answer will vary.

**Page 47**
cat/bat, car/star, house/mouse
Rest of answer will vary.

## Page 48
mop, top, stop, shop
can, fan, van, tan
The **o** has a short vowel
sound.
The **a** has a short vowel
sound.
Each set of words rhymes.

## Page 49
dog/log, bun/sun, bug/mug,
tree/knee
Rest of answer will vary.

## Page 50
wet, net, pet, set
wish, fish, dish

## Page 51
The fish can swim in
the pond.
The man hit the ball with
the bat.
Rest of answer will vary.

## Page 52
Zip up your jacket and we will
go to the zoo.
I think there is a zebra there.
Rest of answer will vary.

## Page 53
The boy sat on the rug with
his cat.
The girl and the puppy ran
into the room.
Rest of answer will vary.

## Page 54
A man went for a walk in
the park.
It was dark and he fell into
a hole.
Rest of answer will vary.

## Page 55
The mice like to skate on
the ice.
They have fun in the snow,
but it is cold.
Rest of answer will vary.

## Page 56
The queen is being quiet.
She hides a quarter under
the quilt.
Rest of answer will vary.

## Page 57
Answers will vary.

## Page 58
Answers will vary.

## Page 59
Answers will vary.

## Page 60
Answers will vary.

**Other**

# books that will help develop your child's gifts and talents

### Workbooks:
- Reading (4-6) $3.95
- Math (4-6) $3.95
- Language Arts (4-6) $3.95
- Puzzles & Games for
  Reading and Math (4-6) $3.95
- Puzzles & Games for
  Critical and Creative Thinking (4-6) $3.95
- Reading Book Two (4-6) $3.95
- Math Book Two (4-6) $3.95
- Phonics (4-6) $4.95
- Reading (6-8) $3.95
- Math (6-8) $3.95
- Language Arts (6-8) $3.95
- Puzzles & Games for
  Reading and Math (6-8) $3.95
- Puzzles & Games for
  Critical and Creative Thinking (6-8) $3.95
- Puzzles & Games for
  Reading and Math, Book Two (6-8) $3.95
- Phonics (6-8) $4.95

### Reference Workbooks:
- Word Book (4-6) $3.95
- Almanac (6-8) $3.95

*Over 6 million sold!*

- Atlas (6-8) $3.95
- Dictionary (6-8) $3.95

### Story Starters:
- My First Stories (6-8) $3.95
- Stories About Me (6-8) $3.95

### Question & Answer Books:
- The Gifted & Talented® Question & Answer
  Book for Ages 4-6 $5.95
- The Gifted & Talented® Question & Answer
  Book for Ages 6-8 $5.95

### Drawing Books:
- Learn to Draw (6 and up) $5.95

### Readers:
- Double the Trouble (6-8) $7.95
- Time for Bed (6-8) $7.95

### For Parents:
- How to Develop Your Child's Gifts and
  Talents During the Elementary Years $11.95
- How to Develop Your Child's Gifts and
  Talents in Math $12.95
- How to Develop Your Child's Gifts and
  Talents in Reading $12.95

........................................................................

*Available where good books are sold!* **or** *Send a check or money order, plus shipping charges, to:*

Department JH
Lowell House
2029 Century Park East, Suite 3290
Los Angeles, CA 90067

*For special or bulk sales, call* (800) 552-7551, EXT 112

*Handy Worksheet*

**Note:** Minimum order of three titles. **On a separate piece of paper,**
please specify exact titles and ages and include a breakdown of costs, as follows:

........................................................................

| (# of books) _____ | x $3.95 | = _____ | **(Subtotal)** | = _____ |
| (# of books) _____ | x $4.95 | = _____ | *California residents* | |
| (# of books) _____ | x $5.95 | = _____ | *add 8.25% sales tax* | = _____ |
| (# of books) _____ | x $7.95 | = _____ | **Shipping charges** | |
| (# of books) _____ | x $11.95 | = _____ | (# of books) ____ x $1.00/ book | = _____ |
| (# of books) _____ | x $12.95 | = _____ | **Total cost** | = _____ |